WILD! Exploring Animal Habitats

CREATURES IN A
DARK
CAVE

Francine Topacio

PowerKiDS
press

New York

Published in 2020 by The Rosen Publishing Group, Inc.
29 East 21st Street, New York, NY 10010

Editor: Elizabeth Krajnik
Book Design: Reann Nye

Photo Credits: Cover Johner Images/Getty Images; Series Art LemonyPo/Shutterstock.com; p. 5 IrinaK/Shutterstock.com; p. 6 HamsterMan/Shutterstock.com; p. 7 Hendrasu/Shutterstock.com; p. 8 Matthew L Niemiller/Shutterstock.com; p. 9 JURE MAKOVEC/AFP/Getty Images; p. 10 Vladimir Wrangel/Shutterstock.com; p. 11 Jennifer Idol/Stocktrek Images/Getty Images; p. 12 Braden Powell/Shutterstock.com; p. 13 Jason Patrick Ross/Shutterstock.com; p. 15 Tukkatar/Shutterstock.com; p. 16 Ivan Kuzmin/Shutterstock.com; p. 17 Alexander Pink/Shutterstock.com; p. 19 Radius Images/Getty Images Plus/Getty Images; p. 20 Carsten Peter/National Geographic Image Collection/Getty Images; p. 21 Stephane Bidouze/Shutterstock.com; p. 22 Christian Reinwald/Shutterstock.com.

Library of Congress Cataloging-in-Publication Data

Names: Topacio, Francine, author.
Title: Creatures in a dark cave / Francine Topacio.
Description: New York : PowerKids Press, [2020] | Series: Wild! Exploring animal habitats | Includes index.
Identifiers: LCCN 2019003015| ISBN 9781725304291 (paperback) | ISBN 9781725304284 (library bound) | ISBN 9781725304307 (6 pack)
Subjects: LCSH: Cave animals–Juvenile literature. | Habitat (Ecology)–Juvenile literature.
Classification: LCC QL117 .T67 2020 | DDC 591.75/84–dc23
LC record available at https://lccn.loc.gov/2019003015

Manufactured in the United States of America

CPSIA Compliance Information: Batch #CSPK19. For Further Information contact Rosen Publishing, New York, New York at 1-800-237-9932.

CONTENTS

CAVE BASICS

Caves are large, hollow places formed by natural **processes** in the side of a hill or cliff, or underground. These dark places are home to life and rock forms many people have never had the chance to see. Because the sun's rays can't reach very far inside caves, they're usually cool inside. Caves can also be formed from ice.

While some caves are big, others are somewhat small. To be considered a cave, the opening must be large enough for a person to fit inside. Caves may have rooms the size of several football fields or thousands of miles (km) of tunnels.

Creature Corner

Jaguar bones have been found inside Lookout Mountain Cave in Chattanooga, Tennessee. Bones from deer, fox, salamanders, and woodchucks have also been found inside the cave.

Ruby Falls inside Lookout Mountain Cave is the tallest and deepest underground waterfall people can visit in the United States.

5

CAVE DWELLING

Several different species, or kinds, of animals dwell, or live, in caves. These animals have adapted, or changed, to live better in cave **habitats**, which are often dark, cold, and wet.

Creature Corner

Some animals are **endemic** to underground habitats, such as those found in caves. These animals are called troglobionts, or troglobites, which means cave dwelling.

MEXICAN BLIND CAVEFISH

Bats belong to a group of cave dwellers called trogloxenes, subtroglophiles, or cave guests. They live in caves more of the time than cave visitors, but must go outside to find food.

Some cave-dwelling animals live near a cave's opening where there's light and warmth from the sun. Others live deep inside the cave, where there's no light. Some of these animals live under rocks on the cave floor or hide in cracks, or small openings, in the cave walls. Some, such as bats, hang from the ceiling. Others live in streams that run through caves.

TROGLOBITES

Many plants and animals need sunlight to survive. However, troglobites, which are creatures born inside and never leave caves, don't need the sun to live. In fact, troglobites wouldn't be able to survive on the surface of Earth. Small troglobites include bugs, spiders, and flatworms, while larger troglobites include cavefish and salamanders.

Creature Corner

Scientists have discovered more than 7,700 species of troglobites. However, there are probably many more to discover because many caves have never been explored.

PRICKLY CAVE CRAYFISH

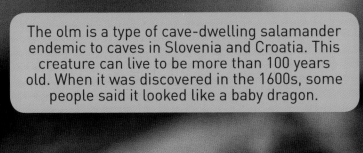

The olm is a type of cave-dwelling salamander endemic to caves in Slovenia and Croatia. This creature can live to be more than 100 years old. When it was discovered in the 1600s, some people said it looked like a baby dragon.

Because caves are dark, troglobites are usually blind and have eyes that haven't grown properly. Many troglobites are pale or white. This is because, without sunlight, there's no need for them to be colored. Troglobites may also have thin skin, longer body parts, and hightened senses.

THE MEXICAN BLIND CAVEFISH

The Mexican blind cavefish, also known as the Mexican tetra, is a species of blind cavefish that lives in underground streams. They are only about 4 inches (10 cm) long.

Food in caves is hard to come by, and the Mexican blind cavefish eats almost anything it can find. It finds food by sensing small **vibrations** from its prey, which are animals it hunts for food.

Mexican blind cavefish are born with eyes, but as they grow up, their eyes disappear and the place where their eyes used to be becomes covered with fat and scales.

Because the Mexican blind cavefish is sightless, it finds its way around by following the walls of the cave. These fish have special body parts called neuromasts that help them sense where the wall is and how far away from it they are.

TROGLOPHILES

Troglophiles are cave lovers. These animals spend all or part of their lives in a cave. However, troglophiles are different from troglobites because they have no adaptations to survive living in caves all their lives. Small troglophiles include beetles, crickets, spiders, and snails. Some frogs and salamanders are also troglophiles.

The color of this cave salamander is much brighter than the olm. This is because it's a troglophile, not a troglobite. It lives near the openings of caves and hides under rocks during the day.

Some troglophiles that live in caves never leave the cave, while others go out at night to find food. Cave-dwelling troglophiles are most often found near the entrance of a cave where sunlight still reaches. Troglophiles like living in caves because they are dark, wet places. This also means that many troglophiles can be found under logs and rocks.

CAVE CRICKETS

Cave crickets are a common troglophile found all over the world. Some species of cave crickets are blind. Adult cave crickets, unlike other crickets, don't have wings. This is because they wouldn't be able to see where they're going in a dark cave. Instead of flying, cave crickets find their way around dark places by moving their long **antennae** from side to side. Cave crickets have long back legs, which allow them to jump high and far.

Cave crickets eat whatever they can find. They eat bits of dead plants or animals most often. They may even eat other dead cave crickets!

Creature Corner

Cave crickets are common household pests. They like to live in people's basements, garages, and other wet, warm, and dark places. They also like to eat stored clothes and blankets!

Cave crickets have a humped back. This is why they are sometimes called camel crickets.

15

TROGLOXENES

Trogloxenes, or cave guests, are animals that live in and around caves, but can't depend on caves for every part of their life cycle. A number of trogloxenes—including cave bears, cave lions, and cave leopards—have gone extinct, or died out.

Creature Corner

Animals that use caves for shelter from predators or the weather are called accidentals. Accidentals include humans, porcupines, and some types of snakes, to name a few.

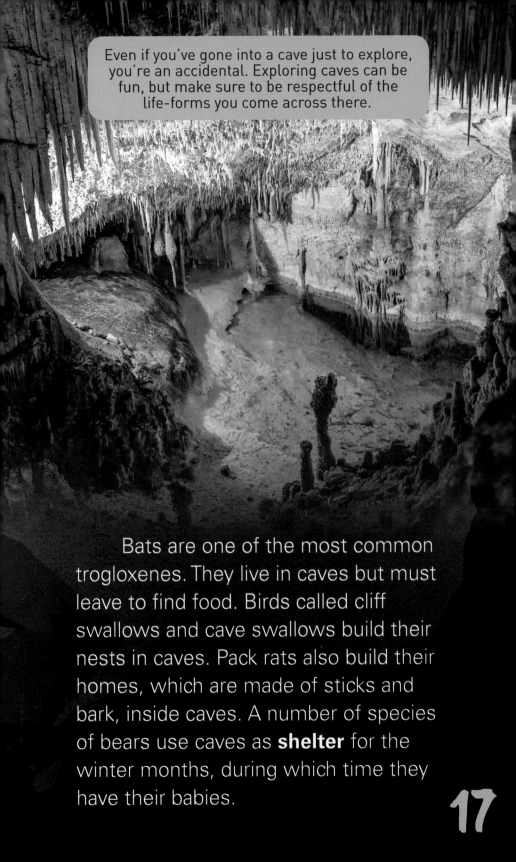

Even if you've gone into a cave just to explore, you're an accidental. Exploring caves can be fun, but make sure to be respectful of the life-forms you come across there.

Bats are one of the most common trogloxenes. They live in caves but must leave to find food. Birds called cliff swallows and cave swallows build their nests in caves. Pack rats also build their homes, which are made of sticks and bark, inside caves. A number of species of bears use caves as **shelter** for the winter months, during which time they have their babies.

17

THE BRAZILIAN FREE-TAILED BAT

Brazilian free-tailed bats are important members of cave **ecosystems**. They roost, or sleep, in caves in great numbers during the day and take flight at night in search of food. Brazilian free-tailed bats control the population of bugs, and just one bat can eat half its weight in bugs every night!

The caves Brazilian free-tailed bats live in are called guano caves. Guano is the name for bat droppings. Animals, such as the guano beetle, that live on the floor of guano caves eat the bats' guano. Flesh-eating beetles eat bats that fall to the floor and die.

Creature Corner

At Carlsbad Caverns in New Mexico, nearly a million Brazilian free-tail bats leave the cave each evening during summer. Many people gather to watch them take flight.

Brazilian free-tailed bats are known carriers of **rabies**.

OTHER CAVE LIFE

Not all plants are suited to growing in caves. Because caves are often very dark and wet, plants such as ferns, mosses, and **algae**—as well as **fungi**—grow well there. Green plants need sunlight to grow and will survive near the entrance of the cave. As you go deeper into a cave, plants get smaller and simpler.

Scientists have found 31 endemic plant species in some of the more than 60 caves they explored in parts of southern China.

In the dark part of the cave, where no sunlight reaches, only fungi and algae can grow. These plants get their power from dead plants and animals or other matter, such as bat guano. Microbes, which are super small life-forms, also live in caves.

21

CAVE SAFETY

Exploring caves can be fun. Caves often have beautiful rock forms and interesting plant and animal life. However, exploring caves can be unsafe if you aren't careful. Be sure to go with an adult and use safety gear. You should always wear proper shoes, a helmet, and warm clothes. Always carry a water bottle, snacks, rope, and a flashlight.

Taking a guided cave tour is a great way to learn more about caves and their life-forms. When visiting caves, you should treat the plant and animal life with respect. Don't leave your trash behind. Respecting cave life is part of having fun!

GLOSSARY

alga: Plantlike living things that are mostly found in water. The plural form is algae.

antenna: One of two or four threadlike movable feelers on the head of insects and crustaceans. The plural form is antennae.

ecosystem: All the living things in an area.

endemic: Growing or existing in a certain place or region.

fungus: A living thing that is like a plant but that doesn't have leaves, flowers, or green color or make its own food. The plural form is fungi.

habitat: The natural home for plants, animals, and other living things.

process: A series of actions, motions, or operations leading to some result.

rabies: A sometimes deadly disease that affects the central nervous system. It is carried in the spit of some animals.

shelter: Something that covers or protects people or things.

vibration: A small, quick movement.

INDEX

WEBSITES

Due to the changing nature of Internet links, PowerKids Press has
developed an online list of websites related to the subject of this
book. This site is updated regularly. Please use this link to access
the list: www.powerkidslinks.com/wild/cave